NATURE UNLEASHED

WILDFIRES

Louise and Richard Spilsbury

W
FRANKLIN WATTS
LONDON • SYDNEY

Franklin Watts
First published in Great Britain in 2017 by The Watts Publishing Group

Credits
Series Editors: Sarah Eason and Harriet McGregor
Series Designer: Simon Borrough
Picture Researcher: Rachel Blount

Picture credits: Cover: Shutterstock: Nico Jacobs; Inside: Alamy: Forget Patrick/
Sagaphoto.com 13; Library of Congress: Posters of the WPA/Christopher DeNoon.
Los Angeles: Wheatly Press, c1987, no. 230 21t; National Archives of Australia: A6135,
K1/3/83/114 11; Shutterstock: Vladimir Daragan 23, Evgenia Sh. 9, Chokchai Poomichaiya
27, Myszka 15, Tom Reichner 4—5, Toa55 7t, Ververidis Vasilis 1, 6—7, Serg Zastavkin
19; Wikimedia Commons: The New York Public Library 17, P199 21, Self 25.

Every attempt has been made to clear copyright. Should there be any inadvertent
omission please apply to the publisher for rectification.

HB ISBN: 978 1 4451 5399 5

Printed in China

MIX
Paper from
responsible sources
FSC® C104740

Franklin Watts
An imprint of
Hachette Children's Group
Part of The Watts Publishing Group
Carmelite House
50 Victoria Embankment
London EC4Y 0DZ

An Hachette UK Company
www.hachette.co.uk

www.franklinwatts.co.uk

Contents

WILDFIRE DANGER

Fire is one of the greatest threats to the world's forests. Fires can spread quickly through wooded areas, destroying everything in their path. Forest fires can move so fast and so violently that they also threaten homes and lives.

How Dangerous?

Some forest fires can be easily contained. Firefighters put them out before they cause too much damage. Large forest fires destroy important wildlife **habitats** and kill animals. People often escape in time but some get injured or killed by the flames or by falling trees. Really big forest fires can burn for days or weeks, producing lots of smoke that can affect people's breathing or even **suffocate** them if it fills their lungs.

Measuring Disaster

Scientists and firefighters work out how to predict when and where forest fires will happen and how to stop fires.

Fires happen when it is hot and dry. They are spread by the wind.

Weather forecasters use **satellite** images to predict where lightning might start a fire and where hot temperatures, dry weather and high winds create fire hazards.

Forest fires spread quickly and far because dry plants and plant waste catch alight easily.

Firefighters create **firebreaks** – areas cleared of trees and debris – to stop a forest fire in its tracks.

Fires in remote places are difficult to fight.

Some firefighters drop water or chemicals from helicopters or aeroplanes to put out fires.

It can take forests a very long time to recover from a fire. Some of the trees destroyed by a forest fire can be hundreds of years old.

Natural disasters have taken place since the Earth was formed. People have many ways of deciding what the world's worst natural disasters have been, from the deadliest disaster to the costliest. This book includes some of the worst wildfire disasters in history.

WILDFIRES IN ACTION

Forest fires start in different ways and for different reasons. Most forest fires are caused by people. Either through an accident, a mistake or on purpose, humans create the sparks that cause the worst forest blazes.

Starting Fires

People sometimes start forest fires when sparks from machinery, a bonfire or a fire used to burn and clear land of vegetation blows out of control. Sometimes a careless action such as dropping a cigarette from a car window can start a fire. **Arson** is when someone deliberately starts a fire to cause trouble. Wind can fan small fires, making them bigger and spreading them quickly. The wind also blows sparks or **embers** onto new plants, starting new fires.

Strong winds can force forest fires to change direction, making the fires even more dangerous and unpredictable.

In 2007, Greek firefighters had to work hard to stop forest fires spreading to the capital city, Athens.

Heat and Drought

Many forest fires happen after a heat wave, which is a long period of very hot weather. **Drought** makes the land and plants in a region dry and warm. They then catch alight much more easily if touched by a spark. When a small area of dry grass catches fire, for example, the flames heat any surrounding dry plants even more so sparks can easily set them alight, too.

Fire Creating Fire

As a fire grows bigger, it becomes more and more powerful. It creates so much heat and energy that it spreads faster and further, and consumes even more plants and trees. Forest fires can even create their own winds. When fires heat the air above the ground, the air rises, forming winds.

10 RUSSIA

In 2010, the hottest summer in Russian history fuelled hundreds of fires across the country. The catastrophic blazes burnt around 7,800 square kilometres (sq km) of land and turned the skies dark. The fires themselves killed at least 54 people but no one really knows how many more died as a result of the smoke pollution.

Moscow

Russia

Widespread Fires

The average maximum July temperature for Moscow is around 23 degrees Celsius (°C). In 2010, some regions experienced temperatures up to 44 °C. The high temperatures combined with a severe drought and strong winds whipped up and spread smaller fires that were mostly caused by carelessness, such as dropping cigarettes in dense woodlands. There were nearly 600 fires in total. The blazes began in late July and lasted until early September, spreading close to towns and cities. Smoke trapped everyone indoors, leaving streets empty and schools closed. The fires changed Russia's forests for generations. Oak and ash trees will take centuries to grow back.

On the Record

At least 2,000 homes were destroyed in the fires.

Russia used over 200,000 firefighters, 30,000 trucks and engines and about 200 aircraft to fight the fires.

The smoke cloaked several cities for weeks, causing unhealthy levels of smoke and **smog**.

The centre of Moscow, Russia's capital city, was full of smoke due to the raging wildfires of August 2010.

The smoke and smog made people choke and cough, made their eyes water and caused **respiratory illnesses**.

The smoke covered streets and even got into metro stations deep underground!

Smoke from forest fires around Moscow stopped some planes using the airport.

9 ASH WEDNESDAY

Hot and dry summers make fire a real risk in Australia's forests of eucalyptus trees. On 16 February 1983, some of the worst bush fires Australia had ever seen swept through parts of Victoria and South Australia.

Fierce Fires

By February 1983 the area had suffered 10 months of drought: its driest period on record. Plants were dry, there were high winds and little moisture in the air. On Ash Wednesday, temperatures reached 43 °C. Bush fires broke out over a wide area, caused by tree branches hitting power lines, by sparks from deliberate fires and by other unknown causes.

South Australia

Victoria

On the Record

There were many **spot fires** caused by burning material blown ahead of the main fire. Some spread quickly and joined to form a large fire ahead of the main fire.

A change of wind direction caused fires to alter their course and merge. Most deaths occurred in the hour after the wind change.

The fires killed 75 people, including 12 firefighters, and injured hundreds more. Large numbers of people fled to the beaches to escape the flames.

This school at Mount Macedon, Victoria and around 3,000 other buildings were destroyed by the fires.

More than 16,000 firefighters and 1,000 police officers fought the fires.

8 LANDES FOREST

The most deadly fire in Europe in modern times happened in France, in August 1949, when around 1,300 sq km of forest went up in smoke. To this day, many people know nothing about this mega-fire.

FRANCE

SPAIN

Landes forest

Highly Flammable

The Landes region in south-west France, between Bordeaux and the Spanish border, has a giant pine forest. The trees contain a lot of **sap** called resin, which contains oils that make the trees highly **flammable**. This means that they burn easily, and they catch fire especially well if they are dry. In the summer of 1949, the Landes forest was so dry that 350 fires raged. They spread partly because there were fewer people in the region after the Second World War (1939–45), which also meant there were not enough local firefighters. There was also too much undergrowth around the trees that should have been cleared to slow the spread of fire.

On the Record

Of the 83 people who died in the Landes fire, many were volunteer firefighters and soldiers brought in from across France to stop the blaze.

The Landes forest was made by people. They planted maritime pine trees because they grow well in the warm, moist climate near the ocean.

The towns of Arcachon and Cestas and the village of Saucats were damaged in the fire.

After the Landes fire, the local fire service developed better firefighting techniques. Now they can put out a 2 hectare (ha) fire in less than 5 minutes.

Today, firefighters react immediately to fires in the Landes forest and quickly put them out.

7 BLACK SATURDAY

On 2 February 2009, a series of bush fires swept across the state of Victoria in Australia. These fierce and incredibly hot fires were so deadly that the day became known as 'Black Saturday'.

Heat Wave!

Victoria was experiencing a record-breaking heat wave that February, with temperatures up to 46.4 °C. The area had been suffering a long, harsh drought that had dried out many plants. This made them much more likely to catch alight. In this extreme heat, forty-seven major fires started. They spread across the state quickly because powerful winds blew huge balls of flames called **fireballs** through trees and towns. Since the fires, the damaged areas have been largely rebuilt. However, there are concerns for the safety of people living in zones at risk of fire.

Victoria

AUSTRALIA

Melbourne

On the Record

The flames were so hot, their heat could kill people from 300 metres (m) away.

One fire started with a faulty power pole 60 kilometres (km) north of Melbourne. Winds blew the flames into a forest and on through towns, killing people in their homes.

The fires created winds of 120 kilometres per hour (kph) that snapped trees in half. Flames leapt 100 m into the air.

Some people tried to escape the fires by car, but the flames moved so fast many died on the roads.

The fires killed 173 people and injured 500 more. They destroyed thousands of homes.

Some people died because they stayed in their homes, hoping to protect them. People also thought they would be safe there.

6 MIRAMICHI

CANADA

New
Brunswick

Newcastle

Miramichi

Wednesday 7 October 1825 was a sad day for the people of New Brunswick, in Canada. The great Miramichi fire destroyed a total of 16,000 sq km of land in just 8 hours.

Fire Conditions

The summer of 1825 had been very warm with little rain. Forests in the Miramichi area were especially dry, too, that summer as many trees had died from insect damage. Most buildings were made out of wood harvested from the huge surrounding forest. Conditions were perfect for fires. A large one broke out in a forest in north-western Miramichi, where William Wright was working. He ran into the biggest local town, Newcastle, warning people to flee by beating a drum. Unfortunately, no one listened: they thought it was a thunderstorm.

On the Record

The violently strong winds on 7 October made the fire burn at a rate of 1.6 km per minute.

Many ships moored on the northern banks of the River Miramichi were burnt. Some ships that were escaping accidentally carried the flames to the southern banks of the river.

This drawing shows Miramichi in the late eighteenth century. By 1825, the settlements along the River Miramichi had grown bigger due to wealth from selling wood and animal skins from the forest.

To escape the heat of the fire, many people stood in the river up to their necks.

Heavy rain on 8 October doused the fire. By then, 520 buildings had been destroyed.

Heat from the fire was so intense that it baked potatoes growing underground in the fields!

5 BLACK DRAGON

The Black Dragon Forest got its name because it is a dark, densely packed area of coniferous trees cloaking a mountain range. The Black Dragon fire was the worst fire in China for 300 years. It burnt an area of forest bigger than the size of England.

RUSSIA

CHINA

Black Dragon Forest

A Wall of Fire

In May 1987, conditions in the Black Dragon were unusually dry. There had not been much snowfall the previous winter and spring rainfall had been low. High winds fanned several small fires, which had started accidentally. The fires spread through the forest and joined together, forming an enormous wall of flames. The Black Dragon fire was at its most terrifying on the night of 7 May when over 200 people died, mostly from smoke fumes. Another 250 people were seriously injured.

On the Record

The advancing fire was so intense that it used up lots of **oxygen** in the air as it burnt more and more wood. Fire engines stopped working because there was not enough oxygen to burn their fuel.

On the Chinese side of the River Amur, 60,000 soldiers and forest workers tackled the blaze. They wanted to protect their country's **timber**.

On the Russian side of the river, the forest was left to burn because authorities believed they had plenty more trees in other forests.

Many animals died or lost vital habitats in the Black Dragon fire, including many Amur leopards.

Around 150,000 sq km of mountainous forest were destroyed.

4 MATHESON

On a very dry and windy summer's day in 1916, a fire raged through the forest around Matheson, in Ontario, Canada. This raging inferno measured 64 km across and moved at speeds of 64 kph.

CANADA

Ontario • Cochrane

Matheson

Frontier Lands

The railway was completed to Cochrane, Ontario, in 1908 and settlers moved into the local area. They cleared forests to sell and make things from timber, but also to create space for farms and settlements. This left enormous amounts of 'slash', or unwanted branches, thin tree trunks and other waste on the forest floor. On 29 July 1916 the settlers' usual practice of burning the slash to remove it went horribly wrong. The forest was very dry, conditions were windy, and the fires quickly got out of control.

On the Record

The death toll of the Matheson fire was at least 223.

The Matheson fire was so terrible that for several days it shared Canadian newspaper headlines with news about the First World War (1914–18) raging in Europe.

The fire changed Canadian law. By 1917, Ontario had introduced the Forest Fires Prevention Act. This forced people to prevent, be prepared for and know how to stop future fires.

The fire burnt through timber yards and destroyed an area of 2,000 sq km.

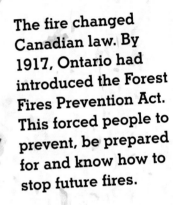

FIRE
WRECKS A FOREST

People failed to control the blaze and it only stopped during rainfall in early August.

The Matheson fire completely destroyed seven settlements, including Matheson and Cochrane, and partly destroyed a number of others.

3 CLOQUET

The Cloquet–Moose Lake forest fires that occurred in Minnesota, in the United States, in 1918 became a devastating natural disaster. The fires spread easily through dry tree stumps and waste that remained after pine forests had been cut down for wood.

Minnesota

UNITED STATES

Cloquet

Forest on Fire

The fires came at the end of a long, hot summer of drought. Trees and stored timber in the area were a **tinderbox** waiting to catch fire. There were already several small fires in the area, when on 12 October sparks from railway locomotives started fires in dry undergrowth next to the tracks. Strong winds fanned the flames and the fires joined up to become enormous. They spread to the Moose Lake-Kettle River area, killing a total of 453 people. Eighty-five more people were badly burnt and 2,100 were injured.

On the Record

The fires lasted 15 hours but moved so quickly that many people were taken by surprise.

More than 52,000 people lost their homes and all their belongings in the fire.

This photo shows the forests in the Moose Lake region today. The fires damaged 4,000 sq km.

Thousands of farms and farm animals were lost.

Smoke from the fires obscured the sun throughout the mid-western and eastern states for several days.

Some people survived by covering themselves with wet soil in farm fields. Other people sheltered in wells, streams, lakes or cellars.

23

2 PESHTIGO

Wisconsin

Chicago •

UNITED STATES

Peshtigo

The Peshtigo fire of 1871 in Wisconsin is the worst forest fire recorded in North American history. Reports vary but it is estimated to have killed between 1,200 and 2,400 people. More than 4,860 sq km of forest were burnt to the ground.

A Fateful Night

There had been scattered forest fires smouldering for days when, on 8 October, winds picked up that made the fires bigger and spread faster. When flames blew from the forests next to Peshtigo towards the city, it was burnt to the ground. The fires destroyed millions of pounds' worth of property and trees grown for timber. By coincidence, there was a great fire in the US city of Chicago on the same fateful night, in which 250 people died.

On the Record

Small **fire tornadoes** travelled ahead of the blaze at around 10 kph.

This mass grave at the Peshtigo Fire Cemetery is a memorial to 350 unidentified victims.

The fires created fast winds that ripped up trees, blew roofs off buildings and blasted barns apart.

There was just one horse-drawn steam fire engine in the area, but nothing else to help people put out the huge fire.

When the fires reached Peshtigo, it burnt quickly because of its wooden buildings and pavements, and sawdust-covered streets.

Many farms and homes were very remote. Before phones, there was no way of warning people.

1 INDONESIA

In 2015, thousands of devastating forest fires burnt the length and breadth of Indonesia. The fires caused huge clouds of smog that spread over parts of Southeast Asia for months.

Slash and Burn

Many of the fires were started by companies and farmers who use fires to burn down trees to clear areas of land. They wanted to use the land to grow palm oil trees and trees for wood pulp to make paper. However, high temperatures and drought had made the land very dry so the fires spread quickly over large areas. **Deforestation** exposes **peat** beneath the trees. Fires in peatland are very hard to put out. In 2015, the fires went on for months. The area will take years to regrow and many people are calling for an end to so-called slash and burn practices.

MALAYSIA

• Singapore

Indonesia

On the Record

There were around 100,000 fires in total.

In some places, people used elephants to carry water pumps and other equipment to put out fires.

The thick blanket of smog resulted in 500,000 people contracting respiratory illnesses. This could cause more than 100,000 deaths.

The smoke from the fires created massive air pollution across Indonesia, Malaysia and Singapore.

The fires devastated many of Indonesia's national parks and deep forests where threatened rare wildlife such as orangutans live.

The fires released **carbon dioxide** into the air, which contributes to **global warming**.

The fires caused billions of pounds' worth of damage.

WHERE IN THE WORLD?

This map shows the locations of the wildfires featured in this book.

Matheson

Cloquet

Peshtigo

Miramichi

Landes forest

ATLANTIC OCEAN

How do you think global warming might increase the risk of forest fires in some areas? Explain your answer.

PACIFIC OCEAN

Read the case studies about the forest fires in Indonesia in 2015, the number one fire in this book, and the fires in Russia in 2010, which are number ten. How do they differ?

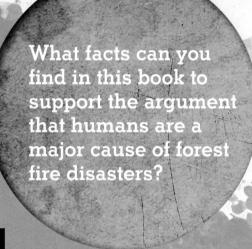

What facts can you find in this book to support the argument that humans are a major cause of forest fire disasters?

Russia

Black Dragon

PACIFIC OCEAN

INDIAN OCEAN

Indonesia

Describe in your own words some of the ways in which people predict fires and work to stop them causing terrible damage.

Black Saturday

Ash Wednesday

GLOSSARY

arson when a fire is lit on purpose with the intention of causing damage to people, land or property

bush fires uncontrolled fires in the trees and bushes of scrubland

carbon dioxide a gas in the air that contributes to global warming

coniferous trees that grow their seeds in cones and have needle-like leaves. They lose and renew leaves all year round, so always look 'evergreen'

deforestation clearing of forests

drought long period without rain

embers smouldering pieces of wood or coal from a fire

fire tornadoes swirling winds created by a fire and usually made up of flame or ash

fireballs balls of fire and fiery gas blown through the air

firebreak a strip of land cleared of plants to stop the spread of fire

flammable burns easily

global warming an increase in the temperature of the Earth's atmosphere caused by human activities such as burning oil, coal and gas

habitats the natural homes of plants and animals

oxygen a gas in the air that animals need to breathe

peat dead plants that have decayed in the ground; peat burns easily and for long periods of time

pollution when the environment is poisoned or harmed by human waste and activity

respiratory illnesses diseases to do with breathing

sap fluid inside plants

satellite an object in space that travels round the Earth

smog a fog made heavier and darker by smoke fumes

sparks small particles of fire thrown from a larger fire

spot fires fires started by flying sparks or embers at a distance from a main fire

square kilometres area; 1 sq km is a square that has sides 1 km long

suffocate when someone dies because they cannot breathe

timber wood prepared ready to build something

tinderbox word used to describe a thing that will catch fire easily

FURTHER READING

Books

Extreme Wildfire (National Geographic Kids),
Mark Thiessen, National Geographic Society

Fire Disaster (Emergency), Chris Oxlade, Franklin Watts

Wildfires (Disaster Zone), Vanessa Black and Cari Meister,
Jump! Inc

Websites

Watch video clips about wildfire formation and the terrible
after-effects at:
www.bbc.co.uk/science/earth/natural_disasters/forest_fire

Click on the fire image to discover how satellites are used to
find and track wildfires at:
www.esa.int/esaKIDSen/Naturaldisasters.html

Find out how to be prepared for a wildfire at:
www.firescotland.gov.uk/your-safety/wildfires.aspx#

Note to parents and teachers
Every effort has been made by the Publisher to ensure that
these websites contain no inappropriate or offensive material.
However, because of the nature of the Internet, it is impossible
to guarantee that the contents of these sites will not be altered.
We strongly advise that Internet access is supervised by a
responsible adult.

INDEX

These are the lists of contents for each title in *Nature Unleashed:*

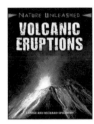

Volcanic Eruptions

Volcano Danger • Volcanoes in Action • Mount St. Helens • Pinatubo • El Chichón • Mount Vesuvius • Santa Maria • Nevado del Ruiz • Mount Pelee • Krakatau • Santorini • Mount Tambora • Where in the World? • Glossary • For More Information • Index

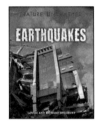

Earthquakes

Earthquake Danger • Earthquakes in Action • San Francisco, 1906 • Nepal, 2015 • Manjil-Rudbar, Iran, 1990 • Peru, 1970 • Kashmir, 2005 • Sichuan, 2008 • Japan, 1923 • Messina, Italy, 1908 • Tangshan, 1976 • Haiti ,2010 • Where in the World? • Glossary • For More Information • Index

Tsunamis

Tsunami Danger • Tsunamis in Action • Flores Sea, Indonesia, 1992 • Chile, 1960 • Nankaido, Japan, 1946 • Tokaido, Japan 1923 • Papua New Guinea • San-Riku, Japan, 1933 • Andaman Sea-East Coast, 1941 • Moro Gulf, Philippines, 1976 • Japan, 2011 • Indian Ocean, 2004 • Where in the World? • Glossary • For More Information • Index

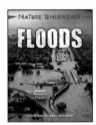

Floods

Flood Danger • Floods in Action • Mississippi Floods • Pakistan Floods, 2010 • Johnstown, 1889 • North Sea Floods, 1953 • North India Floods, 2013 • Vargas Tragedy, Venezuela, 1999 • Bangladesh, 1974 • Yangtse River Flood, 1998 • Ganges Delta, 1970 • Yellow River, China, 1931 • Where in the World? • Glossary • For More Information • Index

Hurricanes

Wind and Storm Danger • Tropical Storms in Action • Great Galveston Hurricane, 1900 • Typhoon Nina, 1975 • Hurricane Katrina, 2005 • Typhoon Bopha, 2012 • Hurricane Mitch, 1998 • Typhoon Tip, 1979 • Hurricane Camille, 1969 • Labor Day Hurricane, 1935 • Hurricane Patricia, 2015 • Typhoon Haiyan, 2013 • Where in the World? • Glossary • For More Information • Index

Wildfires

Fire Danger • Fires in Action • 2010 Russia • Ash Wednesday, 1983 • Landes Forest, 1949 • Black Saturday, 2009 • Miramichi, 1825 • Black Dragon, 1987 • Matheson Fire, 1916 • Cloquet Fire, 1918 • Peshtigo Fire, 1871 • Indonesia, 2015 • Where in the World? • Glossary • For More Information • Index